The Mary Martha Principle

Marvin Swanson

MARY MARTHA PRINCIPLE

Copyright © 2013 Marvin Swanson

All rights reserved.

ISBN: 0-9921046-2-9
ISBN-13: 9780992104627

DEDICATION

A message of dedication to my parents and others like them, who, many times out of their own lack and want, made me rich, by ensuring I always had food to eat and good clothes to wear, and who could always find a place in their hearts for another friend or two to stay for the night. There were always lots of people around the kitchen table on the farm, but it seemed like somehow there was always more than enough to go around. Mom's gravy was second to none, and my dessert usually consisted of more meat and potatoes smothered in her gravy. This was life on the farm in western Canada. Both mom and dad were from large families of eight children; the offspring of hard working European immigrants who had come to Canada to begin a new life with nothing but faith and hope for a better future. They learned to live with little in terms of monetary wealth, but knew the value of family and friends and the difference between a house and a home. Dad and mom's door was never closed to family, friends, or even strangers. The house was not much by today's standards, but it was a home, filled with laughter, as well as tears, music, sports, lots of hard work, many cousins, conversation around the table with one or more of my uncle's or aunts ... and ... yes, even arguments. My dad's side of the family were very political minded. They had strong opinions about who and what they thought constituted good government for the people of our country. Political sermons? I have heard more than most. And I was expected to believe everything I was told. God bless my parents for their faithfulness and commitment to us kids, when many

times it would have been much easier to throw up their hands in despair and call it quits. The message in this book is with them in mind, and all those who know about the hardships of life. My heart goes out to the suffering, discouraged, and disillusioned. My prayer is that the words you read here will inspire you; that you will be encouraged to look unto Him who is both the Author and the Finisher of your faith. There is a better day coming.
Marvin

Adversity? I've known some ... **BUT** ... There's a **BETTER DAY COMING!**

St. Paul's Lutheran Church Odessa Ukraine
Closed by the Communists in 1937 – Pastor Karl Vogel arrested/died in prison camp in Siberia 1943 ... Theophil Ritcher St. Paul's music director arrested and shot 1941 ... St. Paul's burned by arsonists 1976 ... St. Paul's **fully restored and reopened** for Christian Service 2010. A testimony to the devotion (Mary) and action (Martha) taken by her restorers and to the power of the "Mary Martha Principle." HalleluJAH!!!

CONTENTS

	Acknowledgments	i
	Forward	1
1	Mary Martha Principle	5
2	My Shepherd – No Lack	11
3	Green Pastures - Still Waters	18
4	Restoration – Right Paths	27
5	The Valley – No Fear	36
6	Table of Plenty	45
7	Anointing – Full and Running Over	53
8	Shepherds – Goodness and Mercy	60
9	In His Presence	68
10	Anointed For Burial	80
	About the Author	84
	Contact	86
	Restored I Live Again	87

ACKNOWLEDGMENTS

Thank you to my prayer partners in Cali Colombia and to my praying family in Canada. Thank you all for your encouragement and support.

Forward

One morning in 2006 I woke and in a moment of time had a vision. I seen what it would be like to find myself sitting in a chair; staring out a window at age 65 or 70, bankrupt, broke; with no vision or purpose for the future. It was the greatest wakeup call of my life. I will never forget it as long as I live. I immediately responded by repeating these same words in the positive affirmative: "I will die going forward; I will not die in bed or sitting in a chair staring out a window: bankrupt; broke; with no vision or hope for the future." Immediately came to me these words which I believe were given to me by the Holy Spirit: **"It's better to die at sea in quest of the dream in faith still believing, than to die anchored to the shore in fear still dreaming."**

This phrase of words became my motto for living for the next several years. I was deeply in debt. My marriage; and in fact my whole Christian life was all slipping away. The environment of love; God's amazing grace and powerful anointing as I had known it now seemed a thing of the past. I was back in a godless world working on a job with minimal pay, and swearing, cursing, men and women all around me. Reverence for the name of Jesus was like a foreign concept in this sea

of profanity. The job was more like a band aid, barely enough to stop the financial bleeding, and definitely not the cure.
  - exert from chapter four

This message is about God's remedy for disaster through the **"Mary Martha Principle."** God has a plan for total Recovery and Restoration of all things. The remainder of this book is dedicated to discovering this plan, and applying it to my own life. There is no disaster so great that God cannot bring restoration. There is no sickness or disease that is so great that He cannot heal it. There is no addiction or bondage so powerful that He is not more powerful to bring deliverance. There is no darkness so deep that His light and truth cannot penetrate it. We are talking about the One who has power to raise the dead. The One who created the heaven and the earth by the power of His spoken word. Surely He has a plan for me? This plan is revealed here step by step through the **"Mary Martha Principle."**

We will follow a detailed plan based upon Psalm 23. There we will discover that He really is the Good Shepherd who cares for His sheep. You may have heard this Psalm referred to at a funeral, but God's intention is for you to know the power of His Presence in every aspect of your life - all day - and every day of your life. Yes, it's a great Psalm to bring comfort to some grieving soul over the loss of a loved one; but how about the losses you have been experiencing in your present life? Death can wait! Let's talk about the living and being successful and productive in the life we now have. Let's make every day count for both time and eternity.

Jesus said, *"There is only one thing worth being concerned about. Mary has discovered it, and it will not be taken away from her."* Luke 10:42

In this world of devastating losses I invite you to sit at the feet of Jesus with Mary and me, and **discover that one thing which cannot be taken away.**

The **"Mary Martha Principle"** revealed in this book will lead you on a life changing journey of discovery and fruitfulness that you never dreamed possible. Too often we are looking down when we should be looking up. **Martha was looking down at her sister Mary, but Mary was looking up at Jesus.** And Jesus said, this posturing of Mary was a good thing.

Your friend moving forward, as we observe together, the "Mary Martha Principle" for renewed vision, purpose, fruitfulness, restoration, and recovery of things that matter most. God bless you, Marvin Swanson

Psalm 23
New King James Version (NKJV)

The LORD the Shepherd of His People

A Psalm of David.

23 The LORD *is* my shepherd;
I shall not want.
² He makes me to lie down in green pastures;
He leads me beside the still waters.
³ He restores my soul;
He leads me in the paths of righteousness
For His name's sake.

⁴ Yea, though I walk through the valley of the shadow of death,
I will fear no evil;
For You *are* with me;
Your rod and Your staff, they comfort me.

⁵ You prepare a table before me in the presence of my enemies;
You anoint my head with oil;
My cup runs over.
⁶ Surely goodness and mercy shall follow me
All the days of my life;
And I will dwell[a] in the house of the LORD
Forever.

1 MARY MARTHA PRINCIPLE

Luke 10:38-42
New King James Version (NKJV)

Mary and Martha Worship and Serve

38 Now it happened as they went that He entered a certain village; and a certain woman named Martha welcomed Him into her house. 39 And she had a sister called Mary, who also sat at Jesus'[a] feet and heard His word. 40 But Martha was distracted with much serving, and she approached Him and said, "Lord, do You not care that my sister has left me to serve alone? Therefore tell her to help me."

41 And Jesus[b] answered and said to her, "Martha, Martha, you are worried and troubled about many things. 42 But one thing is needed, and Mary has chosen that good part, which will not be taken away from her."

Many people are familiar with this scripture, and it seems like Jesus doesn't care about the service Martha is providing, but this is not the case. We can call this the **"Mary Martha Principle."**

Mary = worship at the feet of Jesus.
Martha = service at the table of Jesus.

What we worship we will ultimately serve. Jesus was simply setting the priorities straight. Before serving at His table?; ... devotion at His feet is required. It is at His feet we receive His instructions for better service. The head instructs the body, not the other way around. Jesus is the head, we are His body of believers. Devotion before service is at the heart of the "Mary Martha Principle." This principle will help guide us through our study of Psalm 23, and the steps towards God's storehouse of abundance, freedom, and success in every area of our lives.

Matthew 4:8-10
New King James Version (NKJV)

8 Again, the devil took Him up on an exceedingly high mountain, and showed Him all the kingdoms of the world and their glory. 9 And he said to Him, "All these things I will give You if You will fall down and worship me."

10 Then Jesus said to him, "Away with you,[a] Satan! For it is written, 'You shall worship the LORD your God, and Him only you shall serve.'"[b]

As usual the devil doesn't tell the whole story. Satan forgot to add that if Jesus worshipped him He would ultimately become his servant. When Jesus responded He said, "For it is written, You shall worship the LORD your

God, and Him only shall you serve." Jesus was establishing the **"Mary Martha Principle."**

In my previous book, "10 DAYS TO TOTAL FINANCIAL FREEDOM," I outlined the importance of understanding the heart of God and laying a solid spiritual foundation for our increase. In essence I was saying "devotion before service." Our service with money is important, but not more important than our relationship with God. For what does it profit a man if he gains the whole world , but loses his eternal soul? Mark 8:36. The point is, God first, me second, as was discussed in greater detail in my previous book. Joseph, in the Old Testament discovered that the **favor of God** was his greatest asset. This is why Jesus could say to Martha, "Mary has chosen that good part, which will not be taken away from her."

The Fiery Furnace – Revival - Promotion

Let's discuss this further. In Daniel chapter three, is a great story about three young Hebrew's who refused to bow down to the King and his false idols. The King was very angry and commanded they be thrown into a fiery furnace seven times hotter than usual. Here was their response …

Daniel 3:16 Shadrach, Meshach, and Abed-Nego answered and said to the king, "O Nebuchadnezzar, we have no need to answer you in this matter. 17 If that *is the case,* our God whom we serve is able to deliver us from the burning fiery furnace, and He will deliver *us* from your hand, O king. 18 But if not, let it be known to you, O king, that we do not serve your gods, nor will we worship the gold image which you have set up."

In essence they were saying, "God first, me second." They were trusting in God as their provider. How many times Have I found myself in a similar position facing a fiery trial? Where is my confidence? In things? Possessions? Other people? Or in God my Savior? Where is my confidence?

Shadrach, Meshach, and Abed-Nego had to face the furnace. There was no escape. They were required to go through the trial. But they did not go alone, for the King said, "did we not throw three men into the burning flames? Look! I see four men, unbound, walking around in the fire, and they aren't even hurt by the flames! And the fourth looks like the Son of God!" (v24-25)

But listen! That's not all! The King then commanded that they come out of the furnace and declared …

(TLB) **28 Then** Nebuchadnezzar said, "Blessed be the God of Shadrach, Meshach, and Abednego, for he sent his angel to deliver his trusting servants when they defied the king's commandment and were willing to die rather than serve or worship any god except their own. **29** Therefore, I make this decree, that any person of any nation, language, or religion[d] who speaks a word against the God of Shadrach, Meshach, and Abednego shall be torn limb from limb and his house knocked into a heap of rubble. For no other God can do what this one does."

30 Then the king gave promotions to Shadrach, Meshach, and Abednego, so that they prospered greatly there in the province of Babylon.

When we put God first, great things begin to happen.

First, they discovered that Jesus was with them in their trial; that the flames had no power over them, and all that perished in the furnace were the things that had them bound.

Second, the three Hebrew men are delivered from their oppressors.

Third, the King who had ordered them to be destroyed in the fiery furnace, repented and recognized the only real god was their God**.**

Fourth, the King commanded all the people of his kingdom to honor the God of Shadrach, Meshach, and Abed-Nego.

Fifth, they were **promote**d and **prospered greatly!**

Note the order:

God first = **Devotion**/Mary at the feet of Jesus/**Favor with God**/Restoration/Revival …

 Me Second = **Action**/Martha at the table of Jesus/**Favor with man**/Promotion.

The first is spiritual/heavenly by nature. The second is

temporal/earthly by nature. The first is our service/ministry to God. The second is our service/ministry to man. Both are necessary and both have merit in their proper place. Both are spiritual. Both are acts of worship when they are under the direction of the Holy Spirit, and the guidance of the Word of God. This is the "Mary Martha Principle." One follows the other as surely as day follows night, and as surely the seasons follow one another in their God ordained sequence.

Devotion at the feet of Jesus before action at the table of Jesus.

This is the Biblical formula for success and prosperity in everything we undertake for the glory of God.

2 MY SHEPHERD – NO LACK

Psalm 23:1 (NKJV)

The LORD the Shepherd of His People

A Psalm of David.

The LORD is my shepherd;
I shall not want.

The LORD is my Shepherd I shall not want/lack.
The LORD is my Shepherd I shall not want for direction.
The LORD is my Shepherd I shall not want for protection.
The LORD is my Shepherd I shall not want for provision.
The LORD is my Shepherd I shall not want for

anointing.
The LORD is my Shepherd I shall not want for peace.
The LORD is my Shepherd I shall not want for joy.
The LORD is my Shepherd I shall not want for love.
The LORD is my Shepherd I shall not want for healing.
The LORD is my Shepherd I shall not want for grace.
The LORD is my Shepherd I shall not want for deliverance from fear, anxiety, addictions, and destructive habits.
The LORD is my Shepherd I shall not want for salvation.

If Jesus is my LORD and my Shepherd then I shall not want. I shall not lack. I shall not be discouraged or disappointed. If Jesus is my LORD and my Shepherd I shall lack no good thing, for Jesus IS the GOOD SHEPHERD who feeds His flock with mercy, grace, and truth.
If the LORD is my Shepherd I shall not want for strength in times of weakness.
If the LORD is my Shepherd I shall not want for encouragement in times of discouragement.
If the LORD is my Shepherd I shall not want for comfort in times of discomfort.
If the LORD is my Shepherd I shall not want for friendship in a friendless environment.

If the LORD is my Shepherd I shall not want for vision and purpose.
If the LORD is my Shepherd I shall not want for wisdom, knowledge, or understanding.
If the LORD is my Shepherd I shall not lack for right standing with the Father in heaven.
If the LORD is my Shepherd I shall not lack for free access to the throne room of God.
If the LORD is my Shepherd I shall not want for answers to my deepest needs and prayers.
If the LORD JESUS is my Shepherd I shall not want for fruitfulness in my life.
If the LORD is my Shepherd I shall not want for abundance of joy and peace and love.
If the LORD JESUS is my Shepherd I shall not want for full assurance of a home in heaven when I leave this earth.
If the LORD is my Shepherd I shall not want for abundance of hope and fullness of faith for He is my true source of all these things and much more.

Psalm 50:10-12
Living Bible (TLB)

10-11 For all the animals of field and forest are mine! The cattle on a thousand hills! And all the birds upon the mountains! 12 If I were hungry, I would not mention it to you—**for all the world is mine and everything in it.**

Question:

If my life is filled with turmoil, unrest, confusion, lack, and want; who is my shepherd?
If my financial world is upside down and inside out; who or what is my shepherd?
If my health and welfare program is in constant disarray; who is my shepherd?
If my world is a turbulent nightmare; who or what is shepherding my life?
If I have an out of control weight problem; who or what is my shepherd?
If sickness and disease are constantly knocking at my door; who or what is my lord and shepherd.

    Could it be that I have placed the cart ahead of the horse? Martha ahead of Mary and misplaced trust? Am I trusting in the wisdom of God and His strength? Or am I trusting in the wisdom of man and my own strength? Have I spent time at the feet of the Good Shepherd? Or do I spend my time on a sofa glued to the latest soap opera? Maybe I spend more time looking inside my refrigerator than looking inside my Bible? Could love for food be my shepherd and the reason I am obese, sick, and in poor health? Could spending more time with my friends over coffee?; or at the shopping mall?; than I do on my job be part of the reason my finances are out of control? The answer to these questions could go a long way to answering my perplexing problem(s).

My good friend, 83 year old, Hernando Meza, from Cali, Colombia, shared the following poem that helps illustrate this further.

"Saul making money, lost his health,
Saul recovering his health, lost his money,
There goes Saul in his coffin."

This is a humorous example of misplaced trust. Unfortunately probably most of us are guilty of this. We need lose neither health or wealth if we are putting God in first place. If our posturing is one of sitting at the feet of Jesus, being instructed by Him, **before we take action,** we will find our efforts multiplied with no more activity than before.

Promotion – Family Income

Let me share the recent testimony of my daughter, Viveca. While reading "10 DAYS TO TOTAL FINANCIAL FREEDOM" she was convicted about the importance of tithing and encouraged by the great promise attached to it if she would obey. Immediately her and her husband, John, agreed to start tithing. They had been wavering in their commitment and giving sporadically, but by making this simple adjustment according to God's Word, they gave God an opportunity to prove Himself to them. **(Read Malachi 3:6-12).** Within two weeks of their decision to place God's Word ahead of man's opinion, John has been promoted to foreman on his job as an electrician, and increased pay. Viveca, a nurse, and stay-at-home mom of two vibrant children, was wanting a part time job 2 or 3 days a week while her son and daughter were at school.

These Things Shall Be Added Unto You

However, she did not have to go looking for the perfect job. **Instead, it came looking for her.** A lady from another church, whom she had not spoken with for several months, contacted her on face-book. The woman informed her that the doctor's office she worked at was looking for a nurse with Viveca's qualifications. This position had been open for a year as they were very selective on whom to give this position to. After a brief conversation the lady said, "Viveca, you are the one we are looking for. The job is already yours. You will love the clinic and the family atmosphere. All you need to do is go through the hiring procedure." Needless to say, Viveca was somewhat surprised, but then she remembered the commitment John and her had made to tithe consistently, and the promise attached to it. A part time job with flexible hours, adding $2500.00 a month to the family income. Not bad! And 100% scriptural. Jesus said, "If we will seek first the kingdom of God and His righteousness, God would add these things unto us." Matthew 6:33.

Mary before Martha. Sitting at the feet of Jesus receiving His instructions before serving at His table. Devotion before action. Viveca could have beat her head against a wall for many days, or even weeks or months concerning the desire of her heart; instead, in a moment of time, with almost no effort on her part, a better answer than she could have expected appeared. Like Mary, John and Viveca chose the good part through their submission and obedience to God's Word, and God chose to give them His increase. Now they will be better equipped to serve at his table, with the combined multiplication in their finances of several thousand dollars a month.

Jesus said, "I have come to give you life and that more abundant." John 10:10.

If the LORD is truly my Shepherd I shall have everything I need.

3 GREEN PASTURES – STILL WATERS

Psalm 23:2
*He makes me to lie down in green pastures;
He leads me beside the still waters.*

I am reminded of a great old hymn that was no doubt inspired by this verse. There are several verses to the song, but here are a couple.

God Leads His Dear Children Along

In shady, green pastures, so rich and so sweet,
God leads His dear children along;
Where the water's cool flow bathes the weary one's feet,
God leads His dear children along.

Chorus:
Some through the waters, some through the flood,
Some through the fire, but all through the blood;
Some through great sorrow, but God gives a song,
In the night season and all the day long.

Lyrics: George A. Young
Music: George A. Young

A Rose Garden - With Thorns

As you can see from the words of this song, not everything in this walk with God is a bed of roses; unless you include some thorns. However, God's ultimate goal for us is a bed of roses *without* the thorns. Thus, the psalmist pictures the LORD as his Shepherd who causes him to lie down in the green pastures, and who leads him beside the still waters. This is the goal of the Good Shepherd. The difficulty lies in the journey to this place of flourishing. We live in a fallen world with many pitfalls and snares. We experience opposition and setbacks, but our Good Shepherd is well aware of all that we will encounter. He brings us into this place of quiet trust where we can truly find our nourishment, and our security in Him and in His promises. The Lord quiets my fears, and I drink from the still waters of His peace that passes understanding in spite of my difficulties, or circumstances. His goal is to calm the wind and the waves beating in my heart before he calms the raging sea that surrounds me. God is a great **"interior designer"** and this is His first priority. The inner man of the heart is where Jesus resides by His Spirit. A heart filled with worry and anxiety is not a fitting habitation for God. Thus, the Holy Spirit must clean house and remove all the debris and devil's dust of fear, mistrust, and unbelief, that has collected there. This is not a place of turbulent waters and barren pastures, but a place of quiet rest; feeding on the promises of God, and drinking from the waters of His grace and truth. God loves His sheep and His greatest desire is for their good and their increase. God's desire is for multiplication. This place of green pastures and still waters is a place of faith, and confident trust in the promises of God and the God who promised. It is a place of unshakeable confidence in God's Word. The blessing begins on the inside by faith and manifests itself outwardly in tangible ways. The intangible, inner working of faith, eventually becomes evident to all. The Apostle Paul discovered this place of green pastures and still waters when he was in prison …

Philippians 4:10-13

Living Bible (TLB)

10 How grateful I am and how I praise the Lord that you are helping me again. I know you have always been anxious to send what you could, but for a while you didn't have the chance. **11** Not that I was ever in need, **for I have learned how to get along happily whether I have much or little**. **12** I know how to live on almost nothing or with everything. **I have learned the secret of contentment in every situation,** whether it be a full stomach or hunger, plenty or want; **13 for I can do everything God asks me to with the help of Christ who gives me the strength and power.**

This is Psalm 23:2 in action. Paul had learned this **secret of contentment** sitting at the feet of Jesus. Like Mary, he had chosen that good part which could not be taken away. Even in prison and suffering for his faith, Paul said he lacked nothing. Paul was content and confident: laying down in the green pastures of knowing Jesus; and drinking from the still waters of His unfailing love no matter what his outer circumstances were telling him.

Preoccupied With Outer Things

Too often we are focused on the outer things and not the inner working of the heart. Like Martha, we are preoccupied with much serving;

forgetting that it is in this place of quiet confidence that God can best perform His miracles. God has called us to serve but on His terms. It is His harvest and we are the sheep of His pasture. By faith we enter in; by faith we drink from the water of God's grace which sustains us; maintains us, and increases us no matter where we find ourselves. The heart of God is for increase and multiplication - *always*. Everything God brings into my life is for this purpose: pruning, cultivating, trimming, remolding; and reshaping. "Herein is the Father glorified in that you bring forth much fruit; so shall you be My disciples," John 15:8.

His Provision According To His Promise

Mark 10:28-31
Living Bible (TLB)

[28] Then Peter began to mention all that he and the other disciples had left behind. "We've given up everything to follow you," he said.

[29] And Jesus replied, "Let me assure you that no one has ever given up anything—home, brothers, sisters, mother, father, children, or property—for love of me and to tell others the Good News, [30] who won't be given back, a hundred times over, homes, brothers, sisters, mothers, children, and land—with persecutions!

"All these will be his here on earth, and in the world to come he shall have eternal life. 31 But many people who seem to be important now will be the least important then; and many who are considered least here shall be greatest there."

Promise Of Great Reward

Giving things and possessions for Jesus sake has promise of great reward; both now in this life, and in the life to come. Jesus also said in another place, "the laborer is worthy of his hire." Knowing God's Word and His promises is the beginning place in finding this location of contentment. Laying down in green pastures is a picture of satisfied sheep. Contented sheep. Well fed sheep. Their needs abundantly supplied.

The Still Waters

Drinking from the still waters speaks of a place of peace and tranquility. Apparently sheep do not like drinking from fast flowing water but shy away from it. When David uses this phrase he is speaking from his own experience as a shepherd of sheep. Still waters. Not turbulent waters. Quiet streams. Not raging rivers. When Jesus rebuked Martha for her much fussing and fuming over dinner, He was not suggesting dinner and her serving were not important; He was simply saying, "quiet down, refocus; look at

Mary, she has chosen the good part which cannot be taken from her ... her peace ... her joy ... her relationship with Me! Dinner can wait! But your relationship with Me cannot! Life is not meant to be a raging river of activity but a place of confident trust and fruitful service under My care!"

Service And Stewardship

Service is an important element of the gospel "and the man who will not work, neither shall he eat." 2 Thessalonians 3:10. Jesus rebuke was not because of her serving. It was because of her fussing; complaining, and her anxiety in her serving. We are all called to serve beginning in our own homes. Working with our hands; being good administrators of our time and money; being good stewards of all God has entrusted us with are all important elements of the gospel. Each of us are called to serve God and one another according to the gifts and talents each of us have received.

Romans 12:3-11
Living Bible (TLB)

3 As God's messenger I give each of you God's warning: Be honest in your estimate of yourselves, measuring your value by how much faith God has given you. 4-5 Just as there are many parts to our bodies, so it is

with Christ's body. We are all parts of it, and it takes every one of us to make it complete, for we each have different work to do. So we belong to each other, and each needs all the others.

⁶ God has given each of us the ability to do certain things well. So if God has given you the ability to prophesy, then prophesy whenever you can—as often as your faith is strong enough to receive a message from God. ⁷ If your gift is that of serving others, serve them well. If you are a teacher, do a good job of teaching. ⁸ If you are a preacher, see to it that your sermons are strong and helpful. If God has given you money, be generous in helping others with it. If God has given you administrative ability and put you in charge of the work of others, take the responsibility seriously. Those who offer comfort to the sorrowing should do so with Christian cheer.

⁹ Don't just pretend that you love others: really love them. Hate what is wrong. Stand on the side of the good. ¹⁰ Love each other with brotherly affection and take delight in honoring each other. ¹¹ **Never be lazy in your work, but serve the Lord enthusiastically.**

Sitting at the feet of Jesus does not exempt us from serving. Being heavenly minded does not exempt us from earthly responsibility. (On the other hand, being earthly minded does not exempt us from taking time to honor God in our daily lives.) Also, having a great prayer life does not give us license to impose upon others. The Apostle Paul worked with his own hands at employment outside the ministry to supply his own needs, and of those who were with him; so that he would be accountable to no one for his daily provision. And to set an example for all believers; repeating the words of the Lord Jesus, **"that it is more blessed to give than to receive."** (Read Acts 20:32-35)

Drinking from the "still waters," may involve taking a job you would rather not do for a season to help relieve a financial problem. If there is no peace, no joy, no still waters, in your present situation: then what must be done to resolve the issue? Paul was not afraid of work. He enjoined work. He simply had his priorities right. Devotion first. Action second. Both are required if I am to drink from this pool of grace.

This Is The Mary Martha Principle.

4 RESTORATION – RIGHT PATHS

Psalm 23:3
New King James Version (NKJV)

³He restores my soul;
He leads me in the paths of righteousness
For His name's sake.

He Restores My Soul

Several years ago everything in my life crashed and burned. Marriage. Ministry. Finances. Relationships. Friendships. Influence. Position. You name it. It died in the crash and burn. This was the result of my own sin of disobedience. I entered into the darkest time of my life. It was like a bottomless pit with no way out. Yet in spite of this I still knew God was with me. The presence of God was still there when I prayed; yet I questioned His love for me on a daily basis. "Jesus, do you still love me?;" was my constant cry. "Do you still love me?"

After Peter's denial, Jesus had asked Peter if he still loved Him ... three times. Each time Peter replied, "Yes Lord, you know I love you."

In my case, I was asking Jesus if He still loved me. I was basing my question on my bad performance instead of on God's unchanging, never failing, unending love and mercy. It took me a long time to recover from this fall from grace. Thoughts of **restoration** were not even in the picture yet.

The Wakeup Call

Until one morning in 2006. I woke and in a moment of time had a vision. I seen what it would be like to find myself sitting in a chair; staring out a window at age 65 or 70; bankrupt; broke; with no vision or purpose for the future. It was the greatest wake up call of my life. I will never forget it as long as I live. I immediately responded by repeating these same words in the positive affirmative: *"I will die going forward;* I will *not* die in bed *or* sitting in a chair staring out a window: bankrupt; broke; with no vision or hope for the future." Immediately came to me these words which I believe were given to me by the Holy Spirit: ***"It's better to die at sea in quest***

of the dream in faith still believing, than to die anchored to the shore in fear still dreaming."
This phrase of words became my motto for living for the next several years. I was deeply in debt. My marriage; and in fact my whole Christian life was all slipping away. The environment of love; God's amazing grace and powerful anointing as I had known it now seemed a thing of the past. I was back in a godless world working on a job with minimal pay, and swearing, cursing, men and women all around me. Reverence for the name of Jesus was like a foreign concept in this sea of profanity. The job was more like a band aid, barely enough to stop the financial bleeding, and definitely not the cure.

Desperation – Prayer - Favor

Out of sheer desperation I prayed and asked God to show me what to do. Through another dream, the Lord showed me that I should apply for a driving position with large trucks. I had been part of this profane world many years before and had no desire to go back into it. A godless world of irreverence; working with people who took more pleasure in using the name of Jesus as a swear word than a praise word. But I thought if this is the only option I have then I must accept it as from the Lord. Obeying this instruction meant upgrading my driver's license. A six week course costing

$4500.00 which I did not have. I also did not have any credit. Neither did I have any family or friends who would be willing to help. This was between me and God. I prayed, "Lord if you do not give me favor with men I cannot do this." Then I made an application for a student loan through my provincial government; thinking there was no way they would accept: given my credit rating and poor income. To my surprise the driving school called me 2 weeks later and said, "you start Saturday." Wow! I could hardly believe it. I knew God had opened this door for me and I better walk through it while I still had the chance. With an attitude of humility and a teachable spirit I told my instructor, "whatever you tell me I will do." Three weeks into my six week course my instructor said, "Marvin, you're ready for the exam and two and a half hour road test. Go for it! I believe you will pass with a hundred percent." Randy was right. I did pass with no mistakes and won the favor of the owner of the driving school as a result.

My Trip To The Gates Of Hell

Denzil Matvichuk, owner of Alberta Big Rig Driving School in Edmonton, got me a job driving a large passenger bus in the Oil Sands at Fort McMurray, Alberta, Canada. One of the largest oil deposits in the world, and one of the last places on earth I would choose to go if there were any other options. If I thought my low paying job in Edmonton was filled with godless profanity? Then the work environment at Fort McMurray took it to a whole new level. I felt like I had been plunged into hell. I thought to myself, "this must be it." But then knowing better I corrected myself and said, "no, this is not hell, but it must be right next door to it." I soon discovered many other people felt the same way about this place. People from all over the world. There for only one reason ... MONEY! It was the same reason I was there. Make as much as you can, as fast as you can, and leave ... and never come back ... was the general attitude. One man said, "this is where you come to pay for your sins," (Catholic purgatory). Another man said, "this is the capitalist equivalent of communist Siberia." I agreed with both. But this was God's answer to my fervent prayer. I determined in my heart I would die on the highway behind the wheel going forward, before I would die in bed: bankrupt; with no vision or hope for the future. This become my home for the next seven years. The **restoration** had begun. Instead of bankruptcy, I was able to pay off $100,000.00 of debt and IOU'S in the first two years. The result of working insane hours. Seven days a week. 112 days between August and December in 2006 with no days off; working split shifts all hours of the day and night. 3800 hours behind the wheel in 2007. 3600 hours in

2008. 15,000 hours in my first five years. Insane? Not from my perspective.

Something More Valuable Than Money

There's something more valuable than money or earthly gain. It's **called dignity, self-worth, self-respect and family honor.** I dropped the family badge of honor: the **baton** that was passed to me by my parents and grandparents, when through infidelity, I fell from grace and broke my marriage covenant of 33 years. In the name of Jesus Christ of Nazareth I determined in my heart that this would not be my lasting legacy. Sometimes desperation is more powerful than faith.

MY MOTTO: *"It's better to die at sea in quest of the dream in faith still believing, than to die anchored to the shore in fear still dreaming."* Repeat this several times a day. Sometimes at night. Sometimes in the morning. Always reminding myself of what it would be like to wake up one day near the end of my life with nothing. My fatigued body would scream, "quit you fool!" But with my heart and soul I would say, "shut up, I'm on a mission," and then ask God for more strength to endure. Then I would repeat my motto one more time. A friend asked, "How did you do it?" I answered, "desperation and pure determination."

I was on the road to **RECOVERY,** and nothing or no one was going to prevent it short of death itself. I declared, *"I'll die on the mountain. I may not reach the top, but if I die, you will find me somewhere on the side looking up. You will not find me at the bottom looking at the mountain; wondering if I could have done it but never made the effort. I will die climbing this mountain. I will not die at the bottom or anchored to my bed in fear."*

I had the family badge of honor in mind.

It wasn't just the financial part. It was everything else which added to the burden. But God is a great God! And faithful! Even in my unfaithfulness God still remained true. He is a great God and Savior! Jesus Christ our Lord! It wasn't just about the restoration of my finances, although that was important, but the **RESTORATION OF MY SOUL!**

He restores my soul;

Psalm 23:3b
He leads me in the paths of righteousness
For His name's sake.

The above testimony is part of this

restoration which was the result of the LORD leading me on **this right path** for **His name's sake.**

From The Inside Out

God works from the inside out. This is contrary to much of our thinking because we tend to want to live by our five senses; not by faith. In the beginning, this "right path" had all the appearance of the "wrong path." At least from my perspective. God does not always lead us down paths that merely appeal to our flesh. Ultimately, this restoration is about the right path of God's choosing and it is for His name's sake. It is about the restoration of our soul; not just our outward treasures. With this thought in mind we can better equip ourselves and prepare for "God's will be done not my will be done." Armed with this attitude of humility we are more apt to submit ourselves to His instruction and recover from our folly much sooner than expected. For God's purpose in our recovery is not merely so we can stand upon our own two feet again, but so that we can be useful in helping many other fallen soldiers stand on theirs. I earned a lot of money in the seven years I spent in Fort McMurray. I own no real estate. I drive a 1989 Mercedes purchased from a friend in need. I have few other material possessions. But I do have a lot of people I was able to invest in besides myself: family members, friends, orphans, etc., as well as several global ministries who are impacting millions with the gospel of Jesus Christ! This is God's Kingdom Purpose for good health, great wealth, RECOVERY and RESTORATION!

These are some of the "right paths" God leads us on for "His name's sake." They are paths that bring glory and honor to Him.

The inner work of restoration begins at the feet of Jesus (Mary), and finds its fuller, outer expression, serving at His table (Martha).

5 THE VALLEY – NO FEAR

Psalm 23:4
New King James Version (NKJV)

⁴ Yea, though I walk through the valley of the shadow of death,
I will fear no evil;
For You *are* with me;
Your rod and Your staff, they comfort me.

The Valley Of The Shadow Of Death

On the fridge door of a friend was a small magnetic sticker which read, *"Everyone wants to go to heaven but no one wants to die to get there."* I found this very humorous but also very true. Life is something we cling too until our last breath. Yet, this is a fundamental principle that relates not only to passing from this life into the next, but also the Law of the Harvest in this life. I am sure many people have heard this scripture read at a funeral; naturally they assume this is the only application it has … for the deceased. This is not the picture the writer had in mind at all. Certainly it has an application for the believer in

Jesus Christ concerning death and eternity; but David, the shepherd, was thinking more in terms of the here and now than he was about a future happening. Going to heaven will be great and is the ultimate goal but in the meantime God has a plan and a purpose for us in this earth realm. This plan involves the Law of Sowing and Reaping, or the Law of the Harvest. This is a universal law established by God Himself. Interesting how some recognize this law and even practice it successfully in their own lives, while at the same time not recognizing the One and Only who established it in the first place.

The Tiny Seed Fears No Evil

This is the message of the tiny seed: which being sown in the good soil beside the still waters in the right place for His names sake, must now pass through the "Valley of the Shadow of Death" in order to release the resurrection life it contains. This is the beginning of the "Miracle of Multiplication." The tiny seed "fears no evil" because it knows the LORD, its Shepherd, is with it: watching, guarding, guiding; every step of the way. The tiny seed understands this is only part of the process in its cycle towards full restoration and multiplication.

"There is no gain but by a loss,
You cannot save but by a cross;

The corn of wheat to multiply
Must fall into the ground and die.

Wherever you ripe fields behold,
Waving to God their sheaves of gold,
Be sure some corn of wheat has died,
Some soul has there been crucified-
Someone has wrestled, wept and prayed,
And fought hell's legions undismayed."
-Samuel Zwemer

The Ultimate Seed

This is the message of the tiny seed. Jesus Himself became a Seed. The Ultimate Seed sown on the cross on our behalf and laid in a rich man's tomb. The ultimate expression of Divine favor and love sown into human experience, and the tragedy of man's sin and rebellion against God. Laid to rest in the cold dark tomb; passing through the "Valley of the Shadow of Death," Jesus, the Ultimate Seed, rose again from this place of death and burial on the third day just as He had said! Praise God!!! HalleluJAH!!! Jesus is alive! Jesus has risen from the dead!!!

"The grain of wheat to multiply, had to first fall into the ground and die."

Jesus, the Ultimate Seed, sowed His own life for the express purpose of reaping a great harvest! I am part of this harvest Jesus envisioned when He was on the cross 2000 years ago. So are you if you believe. The harvest is still coming in worldwide and will continue to do so right up until the time of His second coming. In fact, the effects of this harvest of souls will never end throughout all eternity.

How does this work in my own life?

A Seed Of Compassion

It was a stormy night. The wind blew in all directions; the rain came down in torrents. An elderly man and his wife sloshed up to the desk of a small hotel in Philadelphia. Half in apology he asked: "Can you possibly give us a room? All the big hotels are filled." "Every room is taken, sir," replied the clerk, "But I can't send a nice couple like you out in the rain at one o'clock in the morning. Tell you what: you can sleep in my room." "But where will you sleep?" asked the guest. "Oh, I'll make out," replied the young clerk, "don't worry about me."

Next morning as the guest paid his bill he told the young man who had given up his room: "You are the kind of manager who should be the boss of the best hotel in the United States. Maybe someday I'll build one for you."

Two years later the young clerk received a letter with a round-trip ticket to New York and a note from the guest of that stormy night asking the clerk to meet him in the big city. The old man led the young man to the corner of 5th Avenue and 34th Street. Pointing to a towering new building, the old gentleman declared: "There is the hotel I have built for you to manage."

Almost speechless, the young man, George C. Boldt, stammered his thanks. His benefactor was William Waldorf Astoria. The hotel was the most elaborate of that day, the original Waldorf Astoria. 1

A small act, but a big dividend. *The young manager must have put himself out that night when he gave his room to this elderly couple. We say he* **"died to himself"** *in thinking of others. If he had only known, he was* **putting a seed into the ground;** *that seed would sprout some years later when he would be made manager of the fanciest hotel in New York.*

Jesus says that "the grain of wheat must fall into the ground first before it can bring forth much fruit" (Jn. 12:20). This is a principle in the spiritual life: only dying to ourselves brings forth a harvest of fruit. We find that hard to believe, much harder to live. But it is what Jesus did in letting himself be crucified for us on the cross: for in his dying to himself, redemption was won for all mankind.

-This story adapted from "Grain of Wheat Must Die" by Fr. Gerard Fuller.

This helps to illustrate this whole idea of passing through the "Valley of the Shadow of Death." Sheep are skittish animals and fleeting shadows make them nervous. Growing up on a farm in western Canada I am very familiar with animals that are afraid of "their own shadow." If you are riding a horse that has this problem you better hang on tight, because the next shadow it shies away from may find you sitting on the ground, or worse, standing on your head in uncremonious fashion.

The Law Of The Harvest

Let's illustrate further: I have experienced this sowing reaping effect many times, and in fact, it is a big part of my life. I live by the Law of the Harvest. I practice sowing time and money into the lives and ministries of others. The more that we know and trust God the less we will **shy away from** the idea of giving up something of value.

Returning from doing a series of weekend meetings in a town several hundred kilometers from where I lived, I was pondering what to do with the small offering I had received. I had bills of several thousand dollars and only $200.00 to pay them with. As I prayed asking the Lord for direction, I immediately received His answer: "Sow your seed. What you hold in your hand is not your harvest. It is your seed." The Holy Spirit then instructed me to sow the full amount into a ministry in Ukraine I had helped to establish after the fall of Communism. I said to the Lord, "Consider it done." I stopped at the next town that had a Western Union and sent the full amount as instructed. This was my seed sown in faith and believing in the promise for the harvest. Within just a few days the harvest I needed came in through donations from various givers and the bills were paid in full. Whether it is a small amount like this, or hundreds of thousands, or millions, makes no difference to God. A seed is a seed. And a seed sown in faith gives God an opportunity to bless you with a harvest you cannot imagine. God is not limited in how He can supply our needs when we comply with His master plan of sowing and reaping. I can share countless stories like this from my own personal experience. Whether the harvest comes in this way, or through a new job, or a promotion, or some other way, a harvest is a harvest, accept it and thank God for the increase.

My Seed Money - $4500.00 + Seed Time - 15,000 Hours = A Great Harvest

The income from my job in Fort McMurray, which I shared in a previous chapter, was a harvest for seed I had sown. I have always been a giver and I consider this a big part of my life and ministry. The $4500.00 I sowed into upgrading my driver's license opened a door of reaping I never knew existed. It was like I discovered a new world of income and increase that I had never dreamed about previous. I was complaining to the Lord as I was driving my bus one morning about how much my license had cost me. The Holy Spirit replied, "You are thinking wrong. You are looking only at the cost. You are not looking at the value. *You are not discerning what it is worth.* Instead of asking 'how much does it cost?,'" ask, 'what is this investment worth?" He then said to me, "How much do you earn every two weeks?" I said, "More than $4500.00." The Holy Spirit then said to me, "So how much did your license cost you?" I replied, "Not much! I earn that amount, and more every two weeks." **My $4500.00 investment in 2006 + my investment of 15,000 hours over the next five years turned into a great harvest of more than $545,000.00 + benefits, like health, dental, pension.** Not bad for a farm boy from western Canada, who quit high school to go to work helping his dad and his uncle's with the chores.

The Law Of Sowing And Reaping

I could still be working on my job in Fort McMurray, but God has called me back into fulltime ministry in Colombia, South America.

My income has taken a drastic hit but I am not overly concerned; I know about this Law of Seedtime and Harvest. When I explained to others what I just said to you, some replied, "Wow! I would never pay that much for a driver's license!" They totally missed the point. They **shied away** from the fleeting **"Shadow of Death."** They **shied away** from the idea of having to lay out this kind of cash on the altar of sacrifice and they forfeited their harvest. Some of them are still working at minimal wage jobs and struggling to make ends meet: Instead of enjoying the harvest of a job that pays more than $100,000.00 a year + benefits.

The Trusting Soul Fears No Evil.

The trusting soul places a priority on the Word of God to guard, honor, and protect them. And the Holy Spirit to guide them. They place no confidence in their circumstances, or in their own sense of reasoning, if it is contrary to God's written Word and the witness of the Holy Spirit in their hearts and souls.

For You are with me;
Your rod (Word) and Your staff (Spirit), they comfort me.

This is the Mary (God 1st), Martha (Me 2nd) Principle.

6 TABLE OF PLENTY

Psalm 23:5
New King James Version (NKJV)

⁵ You prepare a table before me in the presence of my enemies;
You anoint my head with oil;
My cup runs over.

You prepare a table before me in the presence of my enemies

A Prepared Place For a Prepared People

Travelling through the "Valley of the Shadow of Death" helps prepare me for this place of plenty. Someone who has been born into this world with a "silver spoon" in their mouth often misunderstands the value of the blessing they have inherited. Simply because they paid nothing for it. It was a free gift. Someone else's sweat, blood, and tears paid for it. The 'someone' who paid the price; not wanting their prize offspring to suffer the same humiliation, and sweat, they had to endure for their success, tries to ease their pain by removing as many obstacles as possible. In contrast, God does not remove all our barriers and opposition in life. Instead, He gives us strength to endure and grace to overcome. There is no place for wimps in God's Army of Believers.

Notice where He prepares a table for us?

In The Presence Of My Enemies.

Psalm 119:65-74
Living Bible (TLB)

⁶⁵ Lord, I am overflowing with your blessings, just as you promised. ⁶⁶ Now teach me good judgment as well as knowledge. For your laws are my guide. ⁶⁷ **I used to wander off until you punished me; now I closely follow all you say.** ⁶⁸ You are good and do only good; make me follow your lead.

⁶⁹ Proud men have made up lies about me, but the truth is that I obey your laws with all my heart. ⁷⁰ Their minds are dull and stupid, **but I have sense enough to follow you.**

⁷¹⁻⁷² **The punishment you gave me was the best thing that could have happened to me, for it taught me to pay attention to your laws. They are more valuable to me than millions in silver and gold!**

⁷³ **You made my body, Lord; now give me sense to heed your laws.** ⁷⁴ All those who fear and trust in you will welcome me because I too am trusting in your Word.

The discipline God brings into our lives is for our own good. Listen to this next word of wisdom …

Hebrews 12:1-13
Living Bible (TLB)

12 Since we have such a huge crowd of men of faith watching us from the grandstands, let us strip off anything that slows us down or holds us back, and especially those sins that wrap themselves so tightly around our feet and trip us up; **and let us run with patience the particular race that God has set before us.**

² Keep your eyes on Jesus, our leader and instructor. He was willing to die a shameful death on the cross **because of the joy he knew would be his afterwards; and now he sits in the place of honor by the throne of God.**

³ If you want to keep from becoming fainthearted and weary, think about his patience as sinful men did such terrible things to him. ⁴ After all, you have never yet struggled against sin and temptation until you sweat great drops of blood.

⁵ And have you quite forgotten the encouraging words God spoke to you, his child? He said, "My son, **don't be angry** when the Lord punishes you. Don't **be discouraged** when he has to show you where you are wrong. ⁶ **For when he punishes you, it proves that he loves you. When he whips you, it proves you are really his child."**

⁷ **Let God train you,** for he is doing what any loving father does for his children. Whoever heard of a son who was never corrected? ⁸ If God doesn't punish

you when you need it, as other fathers punish their sons, then it means that you aren't really God's son at all—that you don't really belong in his family. ⁹ Since we respect our fathers here on earth, though they punish us, **should we not all the more cheerfully submit to God's training so that we can begin really to live?**

¹⁰ Our earthly fathers trained us for a few brief years, doing the best for us that they knew how, **but God's correction is always right and for our best good, that we may share his holiness.** ¹¹ Being punished isn't enjoyable while it is happening—it hurts! **But afterwards we can see the result, a quiet growth in grace and character.**

¹² So take **a new grip** with your tired hands, **stand firm** on your shaky legs,¹³ **and mark out a straight, smooth path** for your feet so that those who follow you, though weak and lame, will not fall and hurt themselves but become strong.

Bible Theology From The Commander-In-Chief

Obviously this is anything but "silver spoon" theology. This is Bible Theology. There's a price to pay if we are going to eat at His table of plenty. This prepared place is for a prepared people who have submitted themselves to the disciplines and instructions required by their Commander-In-Chief. The One who is both the Author and the Finisher, as well as the Chief Example and Chief Administrator of their faith. The disciplines He brings into our lives can only be for our good. It's for His glory, and for our increase. Who ever heard of a winning team with no discipline? Who ever heard of a successful army with no commanding officers? Who ever heard of a successful business with no values or guidelines? Who ever heard of anything, or anyone, who was successful that did not have some form of discipline, or rigors that were followed religiously? We would have to be extremely naïve and ignorant to believe that God's Kingdom is any different. Let's face it. It was God who laid out all these guidelines for success in the first place. Call them success principles of the Universe if you want to? But I would rather give glory and honor where it's due. And call them the Universal Principles of Success which the God who created the Universe set into motion in the very beginning of His creation!!!

What Is My Desire?

If my desire is to become a rocket scientist, but I am a high school dropout, what are my chances of achieving this goal?

If my goal is to become a dentist or medical doctor, but I am presently employed at a fast food restaurant with no further plans for education or upgrading from my current qualifications; what are my chances?

If I am desiring to be an astronaut and be the first person on a distant planet, but I am afraid of flying and have no intention of becoming a pilot or skilled technician; what are my chances of achieving this goal?

My daughter, from age three, had a desire to become a nurse and work with babies and little children. But this desire alone was not enough. It wasn't until she submitted herself to the disciplines and further education required for this profession that she actually was able to accomplish this lifelong goal.

Discipline From Another Perspective

One of the greatest stories I have heard in recent years is the personal testimony of Byron Pitts, in his book, "Stepping Out On Nothing." This book can be purchased at any major bookstore or online from Amazon, Barnes and Nobles, etc. I have the audio book and have listened to it several times. It was a great message of encouragement for me on my road to Recovery. Byron overcame childhood illiteracy and severe stuttering mainly through the encouragement and **disciplines** his mother gave him. His mother did not know how to say "quit." Upon discovery of his illiteracy, she determined they would read one hour a night. If that didn't work they would go for two hours. Through all of his trials of learning to read and overcoming stuttering, Byron learned that his **submission to each new discipline** brought him one step closer to his dream of becoming a journalist. Because of his handicap he had to study each word carefully but through this **discipline** he learned to love words. It was part of the training he would need for his future career as a top journalist and anchorman on major news networks across America. The key word for me in listening to Byron's testimony was the word, **"Discipline."** I had never heard it used in this context before. My concept of discipline was always with the "rod of correction." In my case, this was with a slender green branch from a nearby poplar tree; applied to bare skin when I was a child. But the **discipline** Byron Pitts talks about in his book is the kind of discipline where I submit myself to whatever rules, regulations, concepts, rigors, etc. necessary to accomplish my goal. And to do this with an attitude that whatever it takes I will be willing to do it. **This concept of discipline** was a great revelation for me, and set me free to pursue my dreams and goals with renewed zeal and determination. Thanks to Byron Pitts for his personal testimony and his mother's unyielding determination to see her son succeed in life. Every stumbling block and every obstacle can be turned into a stepping stone if we will **submit ourselves to the required discipline** for the achievement of our goal.

This is the message in "he prepares a table for me in the presence of my enemies."

The Discipline Of Faith

For Byron Pitts, myself, and many others, our biggest enemies are not outside; they are in our own unbelieving hearts. If we never "step out in faith" nothing will happen. The currency of heaven is faith in the promises of God. The Lord has a great banquet prepared for all who will put their faith and confidence in Him, and "Step Out On Nothing But The Word Of His Promise." This is the **discipline of faith** and the basic requirement for entry in to God's storehouse of plenty. **A people prepared by faith in God to inherit the promise of God prepared for them.**

2 Samuel 22:33-37
New Living Translation (NLT)

33 God is my strong fortress,
   and he makes my way perfect.
34 He makes me as surefooted as a deer,
   enabling me to stand on mountain heights.
35 He trains my hands for battle;
   he strengthens my arm to draw a bronze bow.
36 You have given me your shield of victory;
   your help[a] has made me great.
37 You have made a wide path for my feet
   to keep them from slipping.

The discipline of faith learning at the Master's feet (Mary) before the discipline of serving at the Master's table (Martha).

7 You Anoint My Head With Oil
Isaiah 10:27
New King James Version (NKJV)

²⁷ It shall come to pass in that day
That his burden will be taken away from your shoulder,
And his yoke from your neck,
And the yoke will be destroyed **because of the anointing oil.**

The word "Christ" means the anointed One.

Christ (Easton's Bible Dictionary)

anointed, the Greek translation of the Hebrew word rendered "Messiah" (q.v.), the official title of our Lord, occurring five hundred and fourteen times in the New Testament. It denotes that he was anointed or consecrated to his great redemptive work as Prophet, Priest, and King of his people. He is Jesus the Christ (Acts 17:3; 18:5; Matt. 22:42), the Anointed One. He is thus spoken of by Isaiah (61:1), and by Daniel (9:24-26), who styles him "Messiah the Prince."

The Messiah is the same person as "the seed of the woman" (Gen. 3:15), "the seed of Abraham" (Gen. 22:18), the "Prophet like unto Moses" (Deut. 18:15), "the priest after the order of Melchizedek" (Ps. 110:4), "the rod out of the stem of Jesse" (Isa. 11:1, 10), the "Immanuel," the virgin's son (Isa. 7:14), "the branch of Jehovah" (Isa. 4:2), and "the messenger of the covenant" (Mal. 3:1). This is he "of whom Moses in the law and the prophets did write." The Old Testament Scripture is full of prophetic declarations regarding the Great Deliverer and the work he was to accomplish. Jesus the Christ is Jesus the Great Deliverer, the Anointed One, the Saviour of men. This name denotes that Jesus was divinely appointed, commissioned, and accredited as the Saviour of men (Heb. 5:4; Isa. 11:2-4; 49:6; John 5:37; Acts 2:22).

To believe that "Jesus is the Christ" is to believe that he is the Anointed, the Messiah of the prophets, the Saviour sent of God, that he was, in a word, what he claimed to be. This is to believe the gospel, by the faith of which alone men can be brought unto God. That Jesus is the Christ is the testimony of God, and the faith of this constitutes a Christian (1 Cor. 12:3; 1 John 5:1).

Jesus is the Anointed One and He is the One who baptizes believers in the Holy Spirit and with fire. Luke 3:16. Both are manifestations of this anointing. Jesus, the Anointed One releases the anointing through the Holy Spirit when we come to Him in faith confessing Him as Lord with our mouths and believing that God has raised Him from the dead, Roman 10:8-13. The Holy Spirit is the promised Comforter, Counselor, Helper, Intercessor, Standby, Advocate, Strengthener. The Holy Spirit is the Spirit of Truth, John 14:15-16, 26; John 15:26; John 16:13-15 and the anointing which lives inside every believer and teaches us all things, for He is the Truth, and no liar … 1 John 2:27.

He anoints my head with oil … When I come to Him confessing my sin and making Him the Lord of my life, He releases His anointing of peace of mind and joy of heart. The anointing releases me from my fears and anxieties.

John 14:27
Living Bible (TLB)

27 "I am leaving you with a gift—peace of mind and heart! And the peace I give isn't fragile like the peace the world gives. So don't be troubled or afraid.[a]

Peace of mind and heart are fruits of this anointing. Christ, the Anointed One, anoints my head with oil. The oil of peace and joy. The oil of salvation and gladness.

My cup runs over

Jesus doesn't deal in half measures. He fills our lives full to overflowing with His anointing and His blessing. Suddenly the Word of God comes alive like never before. Suddenly I am feasting at a table like I've never known. It's a table filled with splendor. It's a table with plenty of spiritual meat and drink. It's a banquet with more than enough for all who will come. I begin to taste of the goodness of God at a level I never knew was possible. I have discovered a well of living water; a river of blessing that is never ending. It's bubbling up on the inside of me and I cannot contain it. I must share this blessing with others. Anyone who will, may come and freely drink at this fountain of living water.

John 4:14 Living Bible (TLB)
"But the water I give them," he said, **"becomes a perpetual spring within them,** watering them forever with eternal life."

John 7:37-39 New Living Translation (NLT)

Jesus Promises Living Water

37 On the last day, the climax of the festival, Jesus stood and shouted to the crowds, "Anyone who is thirsty may come to me! 38 Anyone who believes in me may come and drink! For the Scriptures declare, **'Rivers of living water will flow from his heart.'"**[a] 39 **(When he said "living water," he was speaking of the Spirit, who would be given to everyone believing in him.** But the Spirit had not yet been given,[b] because Jesus had not yet entered into his glory.)

Note: This is a direct reference to the Holy Spirit which was poured out on the day of Pentecost after Jesus had been raised from the dead and ascended into heaven, Acts 2.

Acts 2:1-21
Living Bible (TLB)

2 Seven weeks had gone by since Jesus' death and resurrection, and the **Day of Pentecost** had now arrived.[a] As the believers met together that day, 2 suddenly there was a sound like the roaring of a mighty windstorm in the skies above them and it filled the house where they were meeting. 3 Then, what looked like flames or tongues of fire appeared and settled on their heads. 4 And everyone present was **filled with the Holy Spirit and began speaking in languages they didn't know,**[b] **for the Holy Spirit gave them this ability.**

1. 5 Many godly Jews were in Jerusalem that day for the religious celebrations, having arrived from many nations. 6 And when they heard the roaring in the sky above the house, crowds came running to see what it was all about, and were stunned to hear their own languages being spoken by the disciples.
2. 7 "How can this be?" they exclaimed. "For these men are all from Galilee, 8 and yet we hear them speaking all the native languages of the lands where we were born! 9 Here we are—Parthians, Medes, Elamites, men from Mesopotamia, Judea, Cappadocia, Pontus, Asia Minor, 10 Phrygia, Pamphylia, Egypt, the Cyrene language areas of Libya, visitors from Rome—both Jews and Jewish converts—11 Cretans, and Arabians. And we all hear these men telling in our own languages **about the mighty miracles of God!"**
3. 12 They stood there amazed and perplexed. "What can this mean?" they asked each other.
4. 13 But others in the crowd were mocking. "They're drunk, that's all!" they said.
5. 14 Then Peter stepped forward with the eleven apostles and shouted to the crowd, "Listen, all of you, visitors and residents of Jerusalem

alike! **¹⁵** Some of you are saying these men are drunk! It isn't true! It's much too early for that! People don't get drunk by 9:00 A.M.! **¹⁶** No! What you see this morning was predicted centuries ago by the prophet Joel— **¹⁷** 'In the last days,' God said, **'I will pour out my Holy Spirit upon all mankind,** and your sons and daughters shall prophesy, and your young men shall see visions, and your old men dream dreams. **¹⁸ Yes, the Holy Spirit shall come upon all my servants, men and women alike, and they shall prophesy.** **¹⁹** And I will cause strange demonstrations in the heavens and on the earth—blood and fire and clouds of smoke; **²⁰** the sun shall turn black and the moon blood-red before that awesome Day of the Lord arrives. **²¹ But anyone who asks for mercy from the Lord shall have it and shall be saved.'**

'You prepare a table before me in the presence of my enemies;
You anoint my head with oil;
My cup runs over."

In Luke 24:49-53 and Acts 1, Jesus had told His followers to **wait in Jerusalem (Mary),** *until* the promised Holy Spirit would come and fill them, and empower them to be bold witnesses in Jerusalem and ultimately the whole world; testifying about who He was **(Martha).** This they did for ten days following His ascension into heaven. Ten days of prayer and *waiting at the feet of Jesus* ... **Mary ... devotion ... reverence and humility before the Lord.** Then ... Acts 2, the outpouring of the promised Holy Spirit and *serving at His table* ... **Martha ... ACTION ... releasing the anointing of the Holy Spirit they had been given.**

The Mary Martha Principle ... devotion before action ... obedience before the blessing ... faith before the fulfillment of the promise!!! HalleluJAH!!!

8 SHEPHERDS – GOODNESS AND MERCY

Psalm 23:6
New King James Version (NKJV)

⁶ Surely goodness and mercy shall follow me
All the days of my life;
And I will dwell[a] in the house of the LORD
Forever.

Surely goodness and mercy shall follow me
All the days of my life

Lamentations 3:21-33
Living Bible (TLB)

²¹ *Yet there is one ray of hope:* ²² *his compassion never ends.* It is only the **Lord's mercies** that have kept us from complete destruction. ²³ **Great is his faithfulness; his loving-kindness begins afresh each day.** ²⁴ My soul claims the Lord as my inheritance; therefore I will hope in him. ²⁵ **The Lord is wonderfully good to those who wait for him,**

to those who seek for him. ²⁶ It is good both to hope and wait quietly for the salvation of the Lord.

²⁷ It is good for a young man to be under discipline, ²⁸ for it causes him to sit apart in silence beneath the Lord's demands, ²⁹ to lie face downward in the dust; then at last there is hope for him. ³⁰ Let him turn the other cheek to those who strike him and accept their awful insults, ³¹ for the Lord will not abandon him forever. ³² Although God gives him grief, yet he will show compassion too, according to the greatness of his loving-kindness. ³³ For he does not enjoy afflicting men and causing sorrow.

Trained "Sheepdogs"

The very character of God is faithfulness, goodness, and mercy. His faithfulness is like a trained Watchman that never sleeps and is always on guard watching over my soul. His Goodness and His Mercy are like trained Sheepdogs, listening for the Master's voice and watching for His hand signals; to lead, direct, and guide me into the green pastures and still waters He has prepared for me. His mercies are new every morning and His compassions fail not. Great is God's faithfulness. This is why I can have confident trust in knowing the Master always has my best interests in mind. Surely these **"Sheepdogs"** will follow me all the days of my life.

A True Story Of Goodness And Mercy

To illustrate this concept I want to share a story with you that was related to me by Eve Goddard, a Catholic woman who attended my church for several years. Eve had grown up in rural Saskatchewan, western Canada. I found this story to be so incredible that I had her repeat it to me many times on several different occasions. I wanted to be sure I heard everything right and had all my facts correct according to her version of its telling.

Louis Vien – Successful Rancher

In the small farming community where she lived with her family was a man named Louis Vien (I'm hoping this is the correct spelling). Louis was a Metis, part French Canadian; part Native Indian. Louis was also a devout Catholic believer; a successful rancher with many cattle, and he was a bachelor. Louis attended his church regularly; was well connected and highly respected in his community. With the fall harvest, there was much work to be done in short order, before the cold prairie winter arrived. Nearby were a family of Eastern Europeon immigrants who had a teen aged daughter. Louis approached the parents; asking if their daughter could be available to cook and look after the household chores for him during the harvest season. He promised to pay her well and that she would be well cared for. The parents agreed, although somewhat reluctantly, because they were losing their free help. The daughter readily agreed because she seen this as a way of escape from a seemingly endless list of things to do without much reward. (You probably already guessed where this story is going? And you are probably right … except for one thing … the details.)

The Proposal

Near the end of the harvest Louis thought to himself, *"this girl is hard working, pretty, healthy, trustworthy, and very efficient in what she does; plus, she does her work without complaint. I think she would make a very good wife."* Again, the parents were somewhat reluctant to give up their eldest daughter on a more permanent basis, because they seen their good, unpaid help disappearing. (I don't recall Eve telling me her name, so let's just say her name is Anna, a good Ukrainian name.) Anna, reasoned in her heart, "how could living with Louis be any worse than living like a slave at home? And besides, Louis has treated me very well over the last several weeks; he has treated me with dignity and not taken advantage of me in any way." As you guessed: Anna agreed to marry Louis! What you didn't guess was she was 18 years old and Louis was 62.

Circle The Wagons The Gossip Has Begun

Needless to say this became the talk of the town. In a small farming community, where everyone knows everyone else, it doesn't take long for the gossip wagons to circle - like covered wagons from a wild west movie. The news spread like wildfire! Tongues were loosed and everyone had an opinion and a reason for such a young girl accepting a marriage invitation from someone forty four years her senior. Louis's two older sisters were part of this circle and they suggested the only reason she wanted to marry their younger brother was for his money. Many others who were part of the local gossip committee agreed and this became the main topic of conversation all over the community.

The Wedding And Eight Children

Neither Louis or Anna agreed to this reasoning and they married. Over the next eight years Anna gave birth to seven sons and one daughter. Eight children in eight years. By now Louis was seventy years old and Anna was twenty six. Being a devout Catholic, Louis took his wife and growing family to church (mass) every Sunday without fail. Eve said to me, *"Marvin, they always sat on the very front row, Louis, Anna, and all eight children. They were the best behaved children in the church and if ever one of them got out of order?; all Louis had to do was look at the disorderly one and immediately the child would stop what it was doing. They loved their dad and mom and the parents loved them. And it showed."*

Tragedy Strikes

Then one day there was an accident on the farm. The children loved their dad and always wanted to be where he was. One day as Louis was working with his tractor one of the boys fell underneath the wheel and was crushed. The death of this child devastated the whole family, but especially Louis who blamed himself for this tragedy. He deeply loved each one of his children and the accident struck deep into his heart. With the help of God's grace, eventually he was able to forgive himself and resume life with the rest of his family; but always remembering with tenderness his son and the accident that could have been prevented.

Eighty Nine - A Miracle And Another Wedding

When Louis was eighty nine years old he was in the hospital in Saskatoon Saskatchewan and dying. His two older sisters, now in their nineties, and still living, suggested to Anna that she pray and ask God to take Louis home to heaven. They reasoned that he had lived a long good life and raised a large family successfully; now it was time to receive his heavenly reward for a job well done. Anna disagreed saying, "Our youngest son is now nineteen and marrying a young lady in Germany. Louis wants to attend the wedding. Instead, I will pray that God restore Louis's health, and allow him to attend the wedding of our son according to the desire of his heart." God answered Anna's prayer. Together, she and her husband attended their youngest son's wedding in Germany. It was a great reunion and a great miracle. Louis had seen each of his children married and starting their own families. Some of them took over the family farm, while others pursued other occupations. All of them were responsible citizens and all of them added value in the place of their choosing.

And That's Not All

Thus ended the story as related to me by Eve Goddard. It was an amazing story of God's grace, mercy and goodness. I said to Eve, "this story should be in the Bible for everyone to read. It's a fabulous, true, modern day story of God's miraculous power and goodness." I continued, "Eve, I promise to tell this story wherever I go. People will be encouraged. Faith and hope will come into their hearts for a better future. It will encourage others to believe God for their own miracle harvest." Then Eve added, **"And that's not all!** Finally, after all those years, the gossip about why Anna had married Louis was stopped: the day Anna prayed for her eighty nine year old husband to be restored in his health so he could attend their son's wedding."

Thank God for this true story as told to me by Eve Goddard.

(Note: At some point I hope to be able to contact some of the members of this family to clarify, confirm, and add any other interesting information to this story. If I have erroneously relayed any of this story I am open for correction from someone who is closer to the family and knows more of the details. As already mentioned I gave the wife of Louis a fictitious name because I don't recall Eve telling her name to me.)

This story helps to illustrate the definition **of "surely goodness and mercy shall follow me all the days of my life."**

Like faithful "sheepdogs" **goodness and mercy** followed Louis and his family all the days of his life. Even in tragedy, God was still with them, bringing comfort in sorrow. In old age God was there to heal and restore and grant the desire of an old man's heart. At age 62, when many people are already retired, or thinking about it, Louis was just getting started on the greatest project of his life; marrying an eighteen year old girl and rearing eight children in the fear of God; teaching them about becoming responsible citizens of their country and valuable contributors to their respective communities; thus following in their father's footsteps.

A Legacy Of Goodness And Mercy

Not only did **goodness and mercy** follow Louis to bring blessing and honor *to him* throughout his long life, but he has left a lasting legacy of **goodness and mercy** which continues to *follow after him,* through his offspring, and many others who were impacted and influenced by his life. I am one of these and now I am relating this story to you.

Devotion before Action - Mary before Martha ... "yes Lord! I'm listening. Jesus I love you. Here I am sitting at your feet ... attentive to Your every word. I've chosen this good part which cannot be taken from me. Thank you Eve! Thank you for taking the time to share this story with me. I'll never forget it. It's etched on my brain and rooted in my heart forever. I'm making good on my promise. I'm sharing it with as many others as will listen.

Surely goodness and mercy shall follow me all the days of my life

9 IN HIS PRESENCE

And I will dwell in the house of the Lord forever

Psalm 16:10-11
New King James Version (NKJV)

10 For You will not leave my soul in Sheol,
Nor will You allow Your Holy One to see corruption.
11 You will show me the path of life;
In Your presence *is* fullness of joy;
At Your right hand *are* pleasures forevermore.

This is a prophecy concerning Jesus Christ and confirmed by Peter on the day of Pentecost, Acts 2:22-33. Because I have accepted Jesus as my Lord and Savior this prophecy also holds true for me … *"Therefore, if anyone is in Christ, he is a new creation; old things have passed away; behold, all things have become new."* 2 Corinthians 5:17.

Not only does Jesus save me from the penalty of hell but also He saves from the corruption of this world; including sickness, disease, and poverty.

In His presence where there is fullness of joy, At His right hand are pleasures forevermore.

John 12:1-8
New Living Translation (NLT)

Jesus Anointed at Bethany

12 Six days before the Passover celebration began, **Jesus** arrived in Bethany, the home of **Lazarus**—the man he had raised from the dead. ² A dinner was prepared in Jesus' honor. **Martha** served, and Lazarus was among those who ate[a] with him. ³ Then **Mary** took a twelve-ounce jar[b] of expensive perfume made from essence of nard, and she **anointed Jesus' feet** with it, wiping his feet with her hair. **The house was filled with the fragrance.**

6. ⁴ But Judas Iscariot, the disciple who would soon betray him, said, ⁵ "That perfume was worth a year's wages.[c] It should have been sold and the money given to the poor." ⁶ Not that he cared for the poor—he was a thief, and since he was in charge of the disciples' money, he often stole some for himself.
7. ⁷ Jesus replied, "Leave her alone. **She did this in preparation for my burial.** ⁸ You will always have the poor among you, but you will not always have me."

A Lingering Fragrance

There is something about the presence of the Lord that is unexplainable. There is something about the anointing that causes hearts to melt in a way like no other. There is something about the name of Jesus that leaves **a**

lingering fragrance once you come to know Him as Mary did. Mary was unashamed about her relationship with Him and wanted the whole world to know. The negative reaction of the disciples her extravagant gift prompted from them had no effect on her whatsoever. Mary is in a familiar position at the feet of Jesus. Only this time she is not waiting His instruction. This time she is pouring out her heart in the form of **an expensive love gift.** It was probably the equivalent of a year's wages. No wonder the disciples reacted like they did. Judas Iscariot reacted the loudest because love of money was a greater weakness for him. This extravagance on Mary's part seems to have proven some hearts and what mattered most to them quickly came to the surface. The real reason Judas was upset was not because he loved the poor and wanted to help them; but he wanted to help himself. In his mind, this expensive perfume being poured out on Jesus head and feet was like sand slipping through his fingers. Mary had a different mindset. Mary was not thinking about herself. She was thinking only about Jesus, and the suffering He was about to endure for her sin and the sin of the whole world. She was not thinking about saving herself or her life savings. She was thinking only about Jesus. And the Lord commended her saying, *"she did this in preparation for my burial."*

Prophet, Priest, And King

There are several anointing's in the Bible. The three we will concentrate on are Prophet, Priest, and King. Samuel was God's anointed as both Priest and Prophet in Israel, 1 Samuel 2:35, 3:19-21. David was anointed by

Samuel as Israel's new King. David was anointed both a Prophet and a King.

1 Samuel 16:12-13
Living Bible (TLB)

12 So Jesse sent for him. He was a fine looking boy, ruddy-faced, and with pleasant eyes. And the Lord said, "This is the one; anoint him."

13 So as David stood there among his brothers, Samuel took the olive oil he had brought and poured it upon David's head; and the Spirit of Jehovah came upon him and gave him great power from that day onward. Then Samuel returned to Ramah.

Notice how the anointing with oil and the Holy Spirit are closely associated. These are two examples of God's anointing coming upon someone for the purpose of serving Him in one or more of these offices. There are many more examples of this but this is for the reader to search out further if you so desire. (Refer back to Chapter 6 "He Anoints My Head With Oil," Easton's Bible Dictionary). In our study of the anointing we will see that in the New Testament, Jesus, the Son of God, is God's Anointed in all three of these offices, as **Prophet** (John 4:19, Hebrews 1:1-3), as **Priest,** (Hebrews 4:14-16), and as **King,** (Revelations 19:16). Why is this important? Because when we come to Jesus confessing Him as Lord and Savior; believing God has raised Jesus from the dead; we are born again. We receive Jesus, God's Anointed, into our hearts and souls. This anointing that is upon Jesus comes upon us, to serve Him in spirit and in truth, as prophets (proclaiming the Good News), priests and kings here on earth.

1 Peter 2:9
New King James Version (NKJV)

9 But you *are* a chosen generation, **a royal priesthood,** a holy nation, His own special people, that you may proclaim the praises of Him who called you out of darkness into His marvelous light;

Revelation 1:6
New King James Version (NKJV)

6 and has made us **kings[a] and priests** to His God and Father, to Him *be* glory and dominion forever and ever. Amen.

This anointing gives us authority; power and presence to proclaim the Good News of Jesus Christ everywhere in the world as His ambassadors. This anointing is a "Teacher" and an "Instructor." Jesus, God's Anointed, was both of these.

What does this mean?

Teachers and Instructors

Let me explain it like this: I grew up in a family of *teachers and instructors.* My dad had four brothers and three sisters. This family of eight children were raised on a homestead in rural Alberta, Canada, near the beginning of the last century; at a time when many of the things we now enjoy, and take for granted were simply not available. Things like electricity, radios, television, internet, telephones, iPads, cell phones, etc. Many of these gadgets had not been invented yet, so their entertainment consisted of family things, like sitting around the kitchen table and listening to their parents tell stories to them. Or working with their parents in the fields, doing chores, working in the garden, working with their mom in the kitchen, or doing house work, etc. All the time talking and sharing stories. My grandpa used to love telling stories about the "old country," as he called it, his native Sweden. Naturally, his children, who had never been much farther than the nearest town for grocery shopping eight miles away, were intrigued as they listened to these stories about this far away land somewhere across a big ocean. You can imagine they asked a million questions about what life was like there in the "old country." Needless to say these stories became deeply ingrained in them and every detail was important to them. So much so that when they retold these stories, no matter how often, or how many times, the story was always predictably exactly the same each time. In fact, as an avid listener I could tell you exactly what the next phrase in each story would be.

Great Story Tellers

All of my aunts and uncles were great story tellers as a result of their upbringing but the greatest of these was my Uncle Henning Swanson. Not only was Uncle Henning a great story teller but he loved to tell stories. And, the more often the better. His stories always seemed to have a sense of humor and were always entertaining. Most of his stories ended with him laughing and saying, "But that was twenty years ago." As a teenager I thought this was hilarious … "Twenty years ago," I thought? "But I'm still a teenager." And then I would laugh along with him. Working with my Uncle Henning was never dull. In

Alberta Canada we have very cold winters. In the spring when the frost comes out of the ground it always brings up rocks and stones buried beneath the surface. This causes a problem for farming. Rocks are hard on machinery and can cause costly repairs as well as reduce crop yields. So every spring they needed to be picked off the fields. Together my dad and three of his brothers farmed a lot of land. I was the only son of age and the family slave. One of my jobs each spring was this work of picking rocks. Probably one of the most boring, thankless, uninspiring jobs on earth. That is, unless you were working alongside my Uncle Henning. He could pick rocks and tell stories with ease and it seemed like he had a rhythm to it. It was entirely predictable. One story would lead to another and with each story I knew what was coming next. Now I had probably heard these stories a hundred times or more, but each time I heard it again, it seemed fresh and new. I learned more about the family history working in the field on a thankless job than any other way. In this way I learned more about my community than I did in school. I knew all the people for miles around, their names, how many in the family, where they lived, and how to get there; even though I had never met many of them personally or physically been to their farms. Uncle Henning's details were astounding! By following his instructions there was not a single farm in my area I could not find and there was not a single person I could not call by name. Talk about an education!

The Original Homestead and Family Roots

It was in this way I learned all the details about the farm my grandfather had grown up on, near a small town named **Glimåkra.** This is a locality situated in Östra Göinge Municipality, Skåne County, Sweden with 1,383 inhabitants in 2010. Probably no more of a population than when my Grandpa left there as a seventeen year old boy in 1900; following his older brothers to the new world - North America. When I visited Sweden in 1971 as a young man in my early twenties, I wanted to visit this farm I had heard about, what seemed like a million times or more. Now keep in mind this was seventy one years after my Grandpa John had left there. I had never saw a picture of the place. All I had ever seen was given to me in the form of **word pictures** by my uncles and aunts, my dad, and grandpa while he was still alive.

Reconnecting

My grandfather's two sisters had remained in Sweden. As a result there were relatives there whom no one of my family in Canada had ever met. The only who had was Grandpa when he returned for a visit in 1954, fifty four years after he had left there as a teenaged boy. My arrival in Sweden in 1971 was a shock to everyone there because they had never heard of me or even knew I existed. But I had an address and a phone number which Grandpa had left after his passing in 1969. The phone number belonged to Sven Bengston, his wife being a first cousin of my dad's. After calling them on the phone and finally being able to explain to them who I was and where I was, they quickly agreed to come and get me. I was at the train station. Sven happily greeted me there and brought me to his home in Malmo. His family were very friendly and welcomed me like their own son. The next day Sven agreed to take me to the farm several hours away where my grandfather had grown up. I had to speak very slowly as Sven's English was not good, and, my Swedish was even worse. The farm had been in the family for more than 300 years but had recently been sold. We had called ahead and the new owners readily agreed for me to come and have a look.

Word Pictures And Tears

As we neared the location of the farm I spotted the house and I said, "Sven, this must be the place. The house looks exactly like it was described to me a hundred times. Same color. Everything." Sven replied, "Yes, this is the farm." As we walked around, looking at the buildings, the fields, etc., I said to Sven, "Please, I would like to look inside the barn." The barn had been of special interest to all of dad's family back in Canada. Because they were farmers, they always wanted their dad to tell them more about how many milk cows, how many pigs, etc. So the barn had been described to me in greater detail than even the house. Now please remember this visit was seventy one years after my grandpa had left and I had never seen a picture, **only word pictures.** I said, "Sven, before we go inside the barn, I would like to describe what it looks like." He looked at me a little bewildered, but said, "Yah, OK, sure." I then described in detail every part of the barn, exactly what it looked like from the descriptions I had heard over and over again. Sven looked at me incredulously, and then with his thick Swedish accent said, "Have you been here before?" I said, "No Sven." Tears welled up in my eyes and I thought, "But it seems like I've been here before. This is my home. My family roots are here. Somehow I have reconnected with my biological roots." I felt overwhelmed and a bit anxious. Now I wanted to go inside and see if the barn was as I described it. It was. Everything single thing. Not one thing was different, even after all those years. It was almost more than I could take, and I thought, "if only my dad, my uncles and aunts could have been here with me now. We could have held hands and hugged and wept tears of joy and sadness together. Tears of joy because we had finally come home to our roots. And tears of sadness because it had taken so long. If only my Uncle Henning had been there with me. We could have laughed and cried together. It was because of him I knew so much in the first place. May God bless him, and all my uncles and aunts who were faithful to pass on the family tradition. It was through their relentless **teaching, instruction, and storytelling,** concerning the things that mattered most to them that I learned the most. I love them all and I can't hold back the tears.

The Family Of God - And I Will Dwell In The House Of The Lord Forever

Time cannot erase the memories. And someday all of us who believe in Jesus, our Anointed, will be reunited around the throne of God with our parents, grandparents, and great grandparents. Some who we never had the opportunity to meet in this life on earth. The **word pictures** will become reality and they will not lie. They will be true to their character just as described. Home at last! Tears of joy because we are finally reconnected with our family roots. And tears of sorrow for why it took so long! We will all gather together one more time. The great big family of God! In His presence where there is fullness of joy! In the throne room of God! This time there will be no more tears of separation. This time we will gather for the last time and all our tears will be wiped away. And we will know that everything was just as it was described ... **word pictures** ... a million times ... inscribed forever on our brain ... imprinted forever in our hearts. Home at last! And we will not be disappointed! We will be happy and thankful for all those who took the time to tell us **the age old story of Jesus and His love ...** over and over ... again and again ... a million times ... the same story ... repeated again and again ... yes, please tell it one more time! In the end, it will be worth it all, because it will be just as it was spoken and a million times more.

Jesus and His love. This is the anointing. It's the family anointing. The family tradition. It is a Teacher anointing. An Instructor anointing. It is relentless in its pursuit of truth and detail.

It is the **anointing of the Prophet** who relentlessly and tirelessly proclaims the message burning in his heart. It is a message for future generations. It is an heritage, an inheritance. It is the family history in vivid 3D, full color, word pictures.

It is the **Priestly anointing** that ministers the family traditions and heritage to its members. It is the anointing that flows from the Head downward to its children consecrating them in the love of the Father and in the unity of the Spirit (Psalm 133), making them of one mind, one spirit, one purpose, sharing the same story, the same love, Philippians 2:10-11.

It is the **Kingly anointing,** releasing the Fathers blessing into the earth realm through His children. It is the authoritative voice of the Father releasing his anointing, his blessing, for their good, and for their prosperity and increase (Read Genesis chapter 48 & 49).

This is the anointing and its purpose. Jesus is the Anointed One and His anointing flows out to us for one express purpose: To **Teach** us more about Himself **(Mary)** and **Instruct** us in His Kingdom Living **(Martha).** The anointing is given for our instruction in preparation for the great family reunion around the throne of God. **The anointing teaches us in <u>word pictures</u> the things pertaining to God's Kingdom.** The anointing of the Holy Spirit is preparing us for the greatest ingathering in human history. The **Holy Spirit** is our **Teacher,** leading and guiding us into all truth. The **Holy Spirit** is our **Instructor** pointing us to Jesus, the Anointed One, the Messiah, God's **"Word Picture"** for the future.

10 Anointed For Burial

Mark 14:8-9
Living Bible (TLB)

⁸ "She has done what she could and has **anointed my body ahead of time for burial.** ⁹ And I tell you this in solemn truth, that wherever the Good News is preached throughout the world, this woman's deed will be remembered and praised."

Mary anointed Jesus body for burial, but in effect this expensive anointing oil was her own anointing for burial as well. In this extravagant act of selfless giving, Mary was in fact giving up the equivalent of her family inheritance and her security for her future. She was in effect saying by her action, *"that nothing in her life held more value than her relationship with the Living God and His Anointed One."* In her mind she was going to the grave with Him. In her mind, nothing in this world held power over her. In her *mind, the cost of the perfume was minimal in view of the worth of her relationship with Jesus, her Anointed One, and the rewards of heaven. "The good part, which could not be taken from her."*

This is the "anointing for burial" in its full scope. And Jesus said to the cold hearted, tight fisted disciples who had rebuked Mary for this selfless act, *"I tell you this in solemn truth, that wherever the Good News is preached throughout the world, this woman's deed will be remembered and praised."*

This is the "Mary Martha Principle" full measure, shaken together, pressed down and running over. It's part of the Family Tradition. (Note: Luke 6:38)

The telling and retelling of this story for the past 2000 years, and the fact you are listening to this story one more time, is proof positive that the Words of Jesus are true and in keeping with this tradition. The anointing of Prophet, Priest, and King, are upon *you* now to share the story with the next generation ... unashamedly, unabashedly; without comprise or apology; without deviation ... over and over again ... in the true spirit of your Prophetic, Priestly, Kingly anointing. All for the glory of God and the increase of His eternal Kingdom. For your benefit and that of many others. Amen! And Amen!

Flowing In The Anointing Here At The Feet Of Jesus – And Here At His Table

Our story ends in a familiar place. Right where it began; at the feet of Jesus. With some variations. Martha is still serving, but no longer looking down at Mary. Mary is still at the feet of Jesus, but now, instead of receiving instruction and being taught by the Anointed One, she is flowing in the anointing of the Holy Spirit herself: giving instruction; teaching the disciples, and in fact the whole world about the value of selfless service.

How? By looking past the cost of her sacrifice and seeing the worth of her object of worship. In this view, Mary teaches all of us a valuable lesson. Our service: in fact our very lives are to be poured out before Him; a sweet fragrance of full surrender to our Lord and King. Our devotion and our service become as one in worship.

Mary and Martha are one - Mary's selfless devotion has turned to sacrificial giving: flowing in the anointing; giving instruction by her extravagant love gift at Jesus feet; **her giving is her act of worship.** Martha's self-serving has turned to worship; serving at Jesus table without complaint; **her selfless serving is her act of worship.** Mary and Martha have become as one in their devotion and their service in an act of worship to their Lord and King..

This is the "Mary Martha Principle"

And I will dwell in the house of the Lord forever!

Mary worshipping at Jesus feet – Martha serving at Jesus table – Lazarus, (you and I) raised from the dead, (1 Thessalonians 4:15-18) seated with the Anointed One, at Jesus place of honor (Revelations 19:6-9)

- The Family Gathering

Anointed for burial - And the fragrance filled the whole house – The family gathering – And this story will be told wherever in the world the gospel is preached – A Word picture forever inscribed on human hearts – The fragrance of the Anointed One and His anointing still fills the house –Serving at His table – Sitting at His feet – A Guest of honor at His table - And we will dwell in the house of the LORD forever.

Marvin

ABOUT THE AUTHOR

As a born again Christian for more than 30 years and a serious student of God's Word: my greatest joy and passion is teaching the great truths from the Bible just as it is written.

My faith in God and His calling on my life has led me to many countries, as a friend to the poor and hurting; involved in various projects ... from delivering humanitarian aid and Bible's in the Russian language, to spiritually starved Ukrainians after the fall of Communism and the former Soviet Union, to supporting orphanages in India and helping 85,000 poverty stricken Soviet Union Jews make "Aliyah" to Israel.

In addition, at the Lord's command, and with His help, the help of my family, and many others, I re-opened, and re-established an old country church which had been abandoned for 10 years prior. I've had my share of poverty, living and ministering to the poor in under privileged areas. And I am absolutely convinced God has a better plan. This plan, for man's blessing and increase, is contained in His Word. God's roadmap for success. I am all for helping the poor and needy, but I am also convinced that God also has a better plan for increase than continual handouts.

This plan is contained in the Word of God. "For I know the thoughts I think towards you, saith the Lord, thoughts of peace, and not of evil, to give you an expected end." Jeremiah 29:11 KJV. In other words, God's plan for the poor, the destitute, and those struggling to survive financially, is to give them a hope and a future.

Praise God! That's what this book and my life is all about. Discovering the plan of God for my own life and helping others find God's better plan for theirs. I am married and presently living in Colombia, South America, where I am ministering to … you guessed it … the poor. I'm telling everyone about the goodness of God and that His plan for their lives is a good one, for increase and multiplication, and not an evil plan for more suffering, defeat and misery. This is the power of the Word of God to set the captives free! Amen!

Your friend for multiplication, increase, and God's very best in your life.

Marvin Swanson

www.toallnations.net

$4500 SEED MONEY + 15,000 HOURS SEED TIME (over 5 years) = $545,000 HARVEST + BENEFITS
(Read Chapter 5 "The Valley – No Fear")
Note: $545,000 Canadian translates - $981,000,000 Colombian Pesos

Contact Information

Company Name: To All Nations

Author: Marvin Swanson

Address: Canada/Colombia

Visit our websites: www.toallnations.net

http://10daystototalfinancialfreedom.ca/home.html

Email: acts29missions@yahoo.com

Phone: 780 747 9051

Facebook: Marvin Swanson

Twitter@SwansonMarvin

Amazon.ca or Amazon.com for orders of "The Mary Martha Principle"

http://www.amazon.ca/dp/B00F7VRFA0/ref=cm_sw_r_tw_ask_IEjBG.0K9FF1R

For orders of "10 DAYS TO TOTAL FINANCIAL FREEDOM"

http://www.amazon.ca/Days-Total-Financial-Freedom-ebook/dp/B00EZROY2Y/ref=sr

Romans 10:8-13 (NKJV)

8 But what does it say? "The word is near you, in your mouth and in your heart"[a] (that is, the word of faith which we preach): **9** that if you confess with your mouth the Lord Jesus and believe in your heart that God has raised Him from the dead, you will be saved. **10** For with the heart one believes unto righteousness, and with the mouth confession is made unto salvation. **11** For the Scripture says," Whoever believes on Him will not be put to shame."[b] **12** For there is no distinction between Jew and Greek, for the same Lord over all is rich to all who call upon Him. **13** For "whoever calls on the name of the LORD shall be saved."[c]

FULLY RESTORED I LIVE AGAIN

Remember my wounded side?
Remember my charred remains?
Remember my bleeding heart?
Remember the ashes?

The season of weeping has ended. The bleeding has stopped. The ashes have been removed. The heart beating with passion and purpose once again. Worship and service restored.

This is the real life story of Saint Paul's Lutheran Church in Odessa Ukraine which I have shared with you briefly, beginning with the picture of its destruction and some of its history on **page iv** at the front of this book. My first view of this once glorious structure in 2005 was its charred remains. I just stood there and stared ... and wept. I wept for several days ... every time I thought about it I wept some more. It was a picture of my own life. Once a vibrant Christian life filled with the Holy Spirit and on fire for God. Now my life was nothing more than marred remains of what had once been something radiant and beautiful, giving glory to God.

   When I first seen the blackened remains I did not know its history. I did not know what was the cause of its destruction. I thought, "maybe it was bombed during the second world war and never repaired?" I didn't know. But I did know what was the cause of my own fall from grace. Sin. The sin of adultery. I thought of many in the body of Christ, who for one reason or another, had fallen and were in similar condition as this once proud structure. It was a sobering moment and one which I will never forget. Later I discovered its true history. This building became a symbol for me. **First,** it was a symbol of my own destruction. I seen myself in every crack and fissure. **Second,** As I stood there weeping the Holy Spirit gave me a prophetic word for its full restoration. Even though this was only a brick & mortar structure, still it symbolized something God was wanting to do in the body of Christ and its wounded soldiers. Through the dedication, devotion, courage, and selfless serving of the Pastor and committed Christians from both Ukraine and Germany the vision for **restoration** has become a reality. 73 years after its closure, a testimony to the faithfulness of God and the Mary (devotion) Martha (action) Principle shared in this book.
Praise God forever and ever! Amen!

THE MARY MARTHA PRINCIPLE

MARY MARTHA PRINCIPLE

www.ingramcontent.com/pod-product-compliance
Lightning Source LLC
Chambersburg PA
CBHW042309150426

43198CB00001B/23